D0417143

SCIENCE SKILLS SORTED

EVOLUTION
AND CLASSIFICATION

ANNA CLAYBOURNE

W
FRANKLIN WATTS
LONDON·SYDNEY

Franklin Watts
First published in Great Britain in 2017 by The Watts Publishing Group

Copyright © The Watts Publishing Group 2017

All rights reserved.

Credits
Series Editor: Amy Pimperton
Series Designer: Emma DeBanks
Picture Researcher: Diana Morris

Picture credits: Alexkalina/Dreamstime: 20t. Andamanec/Shutterstock: 21bl. Marcel Baumgartner/Shutterstock: 12t. catmando/Shutterstock: 5br. CNRI/SPL: 18cr. Paul Crash/Shutterstock: 3bc. Stephen Dalton/NHPA/Photoshot/Avalon: 8b. Andrea Dant/Shutterstock: 18b. DimaSid/Shutterstock: 16c. dovia982/Shutterstock: 11cr. Dziewul/Shutterstock: 12b, 29t. Elliflamra/istockphoto: 10c. Diek Ercken/Shutterstock: 6c. Erni/Shutterstock: 14t. Ex0rzist/Shutterstock: 21bc. Friedemeier/Dreamstime: 22t. Julien Grondin/Dreamstime: 23t. Steve Gschmeissner/SPL/Alamy: 10b.Henrikhi/Dreamstime: 21brl Oliver Hoffmann/Shutterstock: 17t. Dieter Hopf/Imagebroker/FLPA: 5tr.Hugoht/Dreamstime: 22cl.Interfoto/Alamy: 9b.Isselee/Dreamstime: 5tr. Brian A Jackson/Shutterstock: 1, 18t. MCY Jerry/CC Wikimedia Commons: 4tr. Varin Jindawong/Shutterstock: 21bcr. JPL Designs/Shutterstock: 20ca. Kamonrat/Shutterstock: 24bc. Maksim Kazaov, Hein Nouwens, Igor Petrovic,Tristan Tan/Shutterstock: 21c. Kochergin/Shutterstock: 15bl. Vitaly Korovin/Shutterstock: 29b. KTS Design/SPL: front cover. Richard Laskowski/Dreamstime: 9t.LifeTimeStock/Shutterstock: 15t. Lukas ZB/Shutterstock: 11b. S & D Maslowski/FLPA: 14bl. redrawn from de Muizon C, Nature 413. © Macmillan 2001: 14cr. NaturesMomentsuk/Shutterstock: 21t. Nopainnogain/Shutterstock: 26t. Ali Ozgurdonmaz/Getty Images: 13c. Picture Researchers/FLPA: 14bc. Nataly Ponomarenko/Shutterstock: 28b. Alexander Potapov/Shutterstock: 24bl. PrimePhoto/Shutterstock: 16b. Ondrej Prosicky/Shutterstock: 12c. Redline Vector/Shutterstock: 19t. Revers/Shutterstock: 25b. Arie van'T Riet/SPL: 3br. D Roberts/SPL: 24t. Susan Robinson/Dreamstime: 5tc. Andres Rodriguez/Dreamstime: 21br. M Rutherford/Shutterstock: 20cb.Andrew Sabai/Shutterstock: 6cr. Dario Sablijak/Shutterstock: 4bl. Sanpom/Shutterstock: 16t.Kevin Schafer/Minden Pictures/FLPA: 17b. Svetlana Serebryakova/Shutterstock: 27t. Andrei Shumskiy/Shutterstock: 7r. Sombra/Shutterstock: 6t. Maurus Spescha/Shutterstock: 15bc. Sinclair Stammer/SPL: 22b. Stephen Sweet/Dreamstime: 6b. Szeno/Dreamstime: 22cr. Evgeny Tomeev/Shutterstock: 25t. Vlodymyr Tsyba/Dreamstime: 5bl. Thierry Vialard/Dreamstime: 18cl. Olga Visavi/Shutterstock: 20c. vitstudio/Shutterstock: 7b, 27b. whiteisthecolor/Shutterstock: 11c. CC Wikimedia Commons: 8t, 8ca, 10t. David Wingate/Shutterstock: 15br. Martin B Withers/FLPA: 8c. Rudmer Zwerver/Shutterstock: 14cl. Zyancarlo/Shutterstock: 26b.

Every attempt has been made to clear copyright. Should there be any inadvertent omission please apply to the publisher for rectification.

HB ISBN 978 1 4451 5151 9
PB ISBN 978 1 4451 5152 6

Printed in China

Franklin Watts
An imprint of
Hachette Children's Group
Part of The Watts Publishing Group
Carmelite House
50 Victoria Embankment
London EC4Y 0DZ

An Hachette UK Company
www.hachette.co.uk

www.franklinwatts.co.uk

MIX
Paper from
responsible sources
FSC® C104740
FSC
www.fsc.org

CONTENTS

Worlds in **bold** can be found in the glossary on page 30.

WHAT IS EVOLUTION?

Evolution is a process of gradual change. In science, it means the way different types, or **species**, of living things change over time.

The world has millions of different species of animals, plants, **bacteria** and other living things. They have evolved over millions of years to become the way they are today. For example, today's horses evolved from a much smaller animal – *Hyracotherium*.

This diagram shows some of the stages in the evolution of the modern horse.

Equus (modern horse)
1 million years ago
1.6 m

Pliohippus
8 million years ago
1.25 m

Merychippus
15 million years ago
1.0 m

Mesohippus
35 million years ago
0.6 m

Hyracotherium
50 million years ago
0.4 m

HABITATS AND SURVIVAL

Evolution happens because all living things, even if they belong to the same species, are different. Those that are best at surviving in their surroundings, or **habitat**, tend to live longer and **reproduce** more often.

This happens by chance, and is not deliberate. But it means that each species evolves to become better at surviving in its habitat.

Mushrooms have evolved to suit damp, shady habitats.

NATURAL SELECTION

Here's an example of how evolution works.

1. These rabbit kits (babies) are all the same species, but they have slight differences.

2. For example, some might have stronger back legs, and be better at running fast. Faster rabbits are more likely to escape from **predators**, such as red foxes.

3. This means they will be more likely to grow up and have their own babies. When animals have babies, they often pass on their features to them. So rabbits with strong back legs will become more common, while the weaker ones die out.

baby rabbits

red fox

rabbit running

4. Over time, the species changes, and all rabbits become faster runners.

5. This process is called '**natural selection**'. The best survivors are 'selected' by nature.

EXTINCT AND NEW SPECIES

As well as evolving, living things sometimes struggle to survive. This means their species can die out, or become **extinct**.

Meanwhile, more species can develop. Sometimes, one species divides into separate groups. They can evolve in different ways to become two or more new species.

Dinosaurs died out about 65 million years ago.

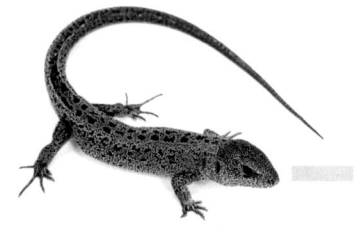

Scientists have discovered thousands of species of **reptiles**, both extinct and living today. They include snakes, lizards and dinosaurs.

THE SCIENCE OF EVOLUTION

The word science means 'knowledge'. So science simply means finding things out. Scientists have been studying our world, and the creatures in it, for thousands of years.

Studying evolution is one of the most important parts of **biology**, the science of life. It helps us to understand why living things, including humans, are the way they are today.

WHAT'S WHAT?

Classification is an essential part of science too. It explains the relationships between living things. When scientists discover a new species, they classify it, and give it its own scientific name in **Latin**. This means that scientists around the world, who speak different languages, always know which species they are talking about.

The axolotl is an **amphibian** related to newts and frogs. Its Latin name is *Ambystoma mexicanum*.

newt

frog

USEFUL KNOWLEDGE

The study of evolution also helps with other areas of science. For example, it helps us fight diseases, such as flu, by learning how disease **germs** evolve. In **geology**, the science of rocks, understanding how life evolved helps scientists work out how old rocks are.

Tiny flu **viruses** can only be seen through a microscope.

6

WORKING SCIENTIFICALLY

In this book, you'll find a range of experiments and investigations that will help you discover how evolution and classification work.

To do experiments, scientists use careful, logical methods to make sure they get reliable results. The experiments in this book use four key scientific methods, along with an easy acronym to help you remember them: **ATOM**.

ASK

What do you want to find out?

Asking questions is an important part of science. Scientists think about what questions they want to answer, and how to do that.

TEST

Setting up an experiment that will test ideas and answer questions

Scientists design experiments to answer questions. Tests work best if you only test for one thing at a time.

OBSERVE

Key things to look out for

Scientists watch their experiments closely to see what is happening.

MEASURE

Measuring and recording results, such as temperatures, sizes or amounts of time

Making accurate measurements and recording the results shows what the experiment has revealed.

WHAT NEXT?

After each experiment, the What next? section gives you ideas for further activities and experiments, or ways to display your results.

EVOLUTION IN ACTION

In the 1800s, two scientists, Charles Darwin (1809–1882) and Alfred Russel Wallace (1823–1913), discovered how evolution worked.

They studied similar living things, **fossils**, and the way farmers change plant and animal species by breeding them. They saw how one species could gradually turn into another or become several new species. Charles Darwin studied birds called finches on the Galápagos Islands near South America. He saw that the different species were similar, but had different beaks for eating different types of food. Darwin realised they must have all evolved from an earlier species.

These are some of the finches that Charles Darwin (top) studied.

THE PEPPERED MOTH

Darwin and Wallace figured out how evolution must have happened in the past. But in the 1900s, scientists realised we could *see* it happening, too. In Europe, a species called the peppered moth began to change its **camouflage**, as smoke pollution from factories made tree trunks and walls darker. Most peppered moths were pale, but a few were dark.

As pollution made surfaces darker, the pale moths were easier to spot against a dark background and birds ate more of them. Meanwhile, more dark moths survived.

The dark moths lived longer and had more babies. Over time, the species became mainly dark. It had evolved to suit its new habitat.

Which of these two peppered moths would be easier for a bird to spot?

pale peppered moth on a tree

SCIENCE EXPERIMENT:

MOTH MODEL

This experiment is a model – a recreation of a real-life situation that works in the same way.

Ask

How does evolution cause a species to change colour over several **generations**?

Moths are a favourite food for lots of birds.

Test

- Use the Internet to find photos of paler and darker tree trunks and rocks and print out several large images.
- Cut 10 dark and 10 pale moth shapes from some of the pictures.
- Pick one player to be the 'bird'.
- While the 'bird' looks the other way, arrange the dark and pale moths on one of the pale backgrounds.
- Give the 'bird' 5 seconds to find and pick up as many moths as possible.
- Try the same test again, but on a darker background.

Observe

Does the 'bird' find less camouflaged moths faster?

Measure

After each test, how many moths of each colour are left behind to survive?

WHAT NEXT?

Do some research to find out if the peppered moth has changed again since environments became cleaner and there is less smoky pollution.

Polluting smoke from factory chimneys was a common sight in the 1800s and early 1900s.

SURVIVAL OF THE FITTEST

You may have heard the phrase 'survival of the fittest'. It dates from 1864, when another scientist, Herbert Spencer (1820–1903), used it to describe Charles Darwin's ideas.

Today, 'fit' can mean strong or in good health. However, in 'survival of the fittest' it does not mean that. Instead, it means the most *suitable*. The living things that survive best are the ones that fit, or suit, their habitat the best.

So, when species evolve, they don't simply get stronger or bigger – they become better **adapted**, or suited, to their habitat. They evolve the most useful features to help them survive.

Herbert Spencer was a famous scientist in the 1800s.

The human eye has many parts that work together so that we can see well. A human retina contains millions of light-sensitive rods and cones.

HOW DO YOU SURVIVE?

In the modern world, it might seem easy for humans to survive. But, like other living things, we have evolved all kinds of useful features to help us stay alive. For example, our eyes are good at noticing movement, which helps us avoid dangers such as an angry animal or a speeding car.

Our bodies tell us when we are hungry or thirsty, and our sense of smell warns us when something is burning. And we have evolved large brains and skilled hands that allow us to invent, make and use all kinds of tools.

REFLEX TESTS

Human and other living things have reflexes, or automatic reactions. Reflexes have evolved because they are useful features that help to keep us safe and deal with danger. These experiments test two of your reflexes.

YOU WILL NEED:

Several people
A ground floor window
Cotton wool balls

 ASK

How do reflexes protect your body and help it survive?

 TEST

- To test the blink reflex, stand one person behind a window. Their face should be as close to the window as possible.
- From the other side, throw cotton wool balls at their face so that the balls hit the window in front of their eyes.
- To test **posture** reflexes, ask the same person to balance on one leg.
- Gently push the person, so that they wobble but do not fall over.
- Repeat the tests with another person.

window
cotton wool ball
blink reflex
posture reflex

OBSERVE

How do people react when you carry out the test? How do their reflex movements protect them or help them? Is it different in different people?

MEASURE

Do some people have faster or slower reflexes than others?

WHAT NEXT?

Think about how these two reflexes could help you survive, especially in **prehistoric** times. What dangers or threats could they protect against?

The blink reflex makes you blink when water splashes on your face.

FINDING FOOD

Living things have evolved ways of finding the best food to help them survive, and avoiding what's bad for them.

For example, many wild animals prefer to drink from running water in a stream. If possible they avoid stagnant, still water, such as in a muddy pond. This is because running water is less likely to contain dirt and germs.

A tiger drinks the fresh water flowing in a stream.

When wolves kill **prey**, they always eat the **organs** and **bone marrow**. Polar bears go for a seal's **blubber**. These animals prefer these parts because they contain the most **calories**, **protein** or essential **vitamins**.

Polar bears feast on a seal, their favourite food.

FAVOURITE FOODS

Humans are similar. We've evolved preferences for foods that contain lots of calories, such as high-fat and high-sugar foods. This is because in prehistoric times, sugary and fatty food was essential for survival. We can also tell when food has gone bad by its smell or appearance. We find it revolting – and that helps us to survive by avoiding food poisoning.

Humans find rotting food, like this mouldy sandwich, disgusting.

YOU WILL NEED:

A computer, printer and paper
A group of people
Pen and paper

SCIENCE EXPERIMENT:

DELICIOUS OR GROSS?

Test your friends' tastes and reactions, to reveal which things humans have evolved to find appealing, and which we find disgusting.

Ask

How do human reactions reveal how evolved preferences protect us?

Test

- Use the Internet to collect pictures of different foods, such as celery, cabbage, doughnuts, pizza, chocolate, bananas and yoghurt, and pictures of mouldy bread, vomit and grass. Print the pictures.
- Show 5–10 people the pictures, and ask them to rate each one from 1 (for disgusting) to 10 (for delicious).

Facial expressions often reveal how people feel.

Observe

How do people react to the pictures? As well as their ratings, look for facial expressions and body movements.

Measure

Add up the scores. Which pictures scored highest and lowest?

WHAT NEXT?

Make a simple graph to display your results, ranking the pictures in order from the most appealing to the most disgusting.

Can you see a pattern? Even though we no longer have to survive in the same harsh conditions as our prehistoric ancestors, many people still like to eat sugary and fatty foods. Can you think how this evolved preference could harm our bodies?

ADAPTING TO HABITATS

Each living thing has evolved and adapted to its own habitat, where it lives, feeds and survives.

For example, a spider monkey lives in rainforest trees. It has a **prehensile tail** for curling around branches, and hands and feet with fingers and toes that are good at holding branches and picking fruit.

A spider monkey uses its tail to grip onto branches.

A mole lives in underground tunnels. It has poor eyesight, but a very sensitive nose for finding food, and big, powerful front claws for digging.

—— European mole

LOSING LEGS

Today's whales evolved from small, four-legged animals. Although they once had legs, they gradually lost them. A smooth body with flippers at the front suited life in the water better. Over time, the back legs shrank away.

pelvis and hindlegs

EVOLUTION EVERYWHERE

Around the world, **biologists** find that where living things have to deal with the same types of habitats and conditions, they tend to evolve similar features. Sometimes this happens even if they are not close relatives. This is called 'convergent evolution'.

flying squirrel

sugar glider

These two **mammal** species look very similar. They have both evolved to glide from trees using loose, thin skin that they can spread out like wings. But they are very different – the sugar glider is a **marsupial** related to kangaroos, and the flying squirrel is a **rodent** related to squirrels and rats.

SCIENCE EXPERIMENT:

CREATURE FEATURES

Predict which kinds of features go with each of the habitats, then check your predictions against the answers. Scientists check their predictions by making observations 'in the field'.

fennec fox

ASK

What features do you think animals will adapt for particular habitats?

OBSERVE

How do you decide which goes where?

TEST

- Research and print out photographs of three habitats: a snowy forest, a hot, sandy desert and the open ocean.
- Look at the set of creature features below, and allocate five features to each of the habitats where you think they will be most useful.

- big ears
- big feet
- blowhole
- burrowing claws
- closable nostrils
- flippers
- furry feet
- golden fur
- inflatable body parts
- sharp claws
- small ears
- thick fur
- torpedo-shaped body
- triangle-shaped tail
- white feathers

MEASURE

Check your predictions against the answers on page 32. How many of them did you get right?

WHAT NEXT?

Compare the features to those that humans have. Why do you think we have so little in the way of fur, sharp teeth, tails, big claws, and so on?

WINNING A MATE

The way species change over time can only work because living things reproduce, or have babies, and pass on their features to them. The main reason one animal has more babies than another is because it survives better and lives longer.

However, there's another way to have more babies, and that's to be the best at finding a **mate**. Many species have features that help them do this, such as the male peacock's tail.

Male peacocks with the biggest and brightest tails are more likely to attract peahens (females) to mate with. Over time, peacocks and many other species have evolved features like these for impressing potential mates, as well as survival features. This is called '**sexual selection**'.

A male peacock's tail feathers have beautiful 'eye' patterns.

A male peacock displays his tail to a passing peahen.

YOU WILL NEED:

Several people
Shoeboxes or shoebox lids
Blue paper, art materials
and other objects
Twigs or wooden lolly sticks
Scissors
Glue, sticky tape
or modelling clay

SCIENCE EXPERIMENT:

BEAUTIFUL BOWERS

Male satin bowerbirds build a bower (a kind of shelter or enclosed area) to impress a mate. Each male decorates his bower with blue objects – feathers, flowers, berries or even blue pieces of litter. Hold your own bower-building contest to see who is best at winning a mate.

Ask

How do bowerbirds make their bowers attractive?

Observe

How do the 'bowerbirds' try to make their bowers the most attractive?

Test

- Appoint one person to be the female bowerbird, who will judge the bowers.
- Give each contestant some time to collect blue decorative objects and materials at home or around the classroom.
- Each contestant should then build a bower from sticks in their shoebox or lid, and decorate it with blue objects.
- Without knowing who made which bower, the 'female bowerbird' should award marks for style, colour and shape, and select the most appealing bower.

Measure

Who was the winner? What type of decorations got the most marks?

WHAT NEXT?

Research the things real bowerbirds do to make their bowers pretty, such as arranging rows of objects in size order from small to large. Can you find out how some other animals display to attract a mate?

A male bowerbird works on perfecting his bower.

GENES AND GENETIC TRAITS

We know that evolution happens because of the way living things pass on their individual features to their babies. But how exactly does this work?

Living things are made up of tiny parts called cells. They have babies, or reproduce, using special reproductive cells. In plants, the reproductive cells make seeds. In animals, reproductive cells make eggs or babies. Tiny single-celled bacteria reproduce by splitting in two, making two new cells.

Dandelions pass on their features inside the seeds they produce.

Chickens pass on their features to chicks in the eggs female chickens lay.

E. coli bacterium pass on their features by dividing in two.

GENES

Cells, including reproductive cells, contain **genes**, which are made of a spiral-shaped chemical called **DNA** (see p. 26). Genes control how a living thing grows and what it looks like. When living things reproduce, they give their offspring copies of their own individual genes in their reproductive cells. This is how features, such as a rabbit's strong back legs or a peacock's big tail, get passed on.

cell

nucleus

DNA

A cell's DNA is in its nucleus.

SCIENCE EXPERIMENT:

TOE TEST

Features passed on in your genes are called genetic traits. They include things like hair colour, height, and shapes of body parts. Children get genes from both their parents, and often share some genetic traits with them. In this experiment, you can test for a genetic trait called Morton's toe.

 Ask

Are biological family members more likely to share a genetic trait than people who aren't related?

Test

- Test yourself and your friends and family for Morton's toe. If you have it, your second toe is longer than your big toe.
- Each person should make a list of their family members, and a list of the same number of unrelated friends.
- They should then ask them all if they have Morton's toe.

This diagram shows a foot with Morton's toe.

This diagram shows a foot without Morton's toe

Observe

Are family members more likely to have the same kind of toes than friends?

 Measure

How much difference is there between the two groups?

WHAT NEXT?

Make two pie charts, one for the group of unrelated friends, and one for the family group, to show the frequency of Morton's toe. You could also combine everyone's results and make a graph to see if they show a pattern.

Repeat the test, but this time compare earlobes. Find out if each person has dangling earlobes, which hang down separately from their head, or attached earlobes, which join to the side of the head at the bottom.

CLASSIFICATION

Life has existed on Earth for at least 3.5 billion years. In that time, millions and millions of different species have evolved. Scientists classify every new species they discover, working out which groups and categories it belongs to.

ONE BIG FAMILY

Scientists think all life evolved from one original life form, which means that all living things are related. Living things *all* work and grow using cells, genes and DNA.

Because species branch off from other species, some are very closely related, and others are much more distantly related. Monkeys are close relatives of humans. Octopuses are more distant relatives, and bananas are really distant relatives.

HOW CLASSIFICATION WORKS

The classification of a species looks a bit like an upside-down pyramid. It shows the categories that a species belongs to. For example, the largest group in this pyramid is a kingdom, such as the animal kingdom, which includes all animals. Animals are divided into over 30 phyla, or main groups. Each phylum can be separated into classes, orders and families, genuses or specific types, and finally individual species.

Kingdom

Phylum

Class

Order

Family

Genus

Species

Look at the simple classification tree on page 23 to see how several branches of kingdom, phylum and class are connected.

Each living thing has its own classification pyramid, showing which groups it belongs to at each level. For example, this is the classification pyramid for a black bear (see right).

Kingdom: Animalia – Animals

Phylum: Chordata – (animals with a spinal cord)

Class: Mammalia – Mammals (warm-blooded animals that have hair and breathe air)

Order: Carnivora – Carnivores (animals that feed on other animals)

Family: Ursidae – Bears (includes the panda, brown bear, black bear and other bears)

Genus: *Ursus* – (includes the brown bear and black bear)

Species: *Ursus americanus* – black bear

GETTING IT RIGHT

Sometimes, scientists classify a living thing in one category, then change their minds as they find out more about it. The giant panda is an example. In the past, it was thought to belong to the raccoon family. Studies revealed it is more closely related to bears like the black bear, and belongs in the bear family, Ursidae.

giant panda

raccoon

SCIENCE EXPERIMENT:

CLASSIFY THIS!

Can you draw and fill in classification pyramids for these three living things, using your own research?

coconut palm tree

seven-spot ladybird

human

SORTING IT OUT

How do scientists know which living things to put where in the classification system? They look at many different things, including: the way a living thing breathes, what it eats, its body shape, limbs, how it reproduces, and whether it has fur, feathers or **scales**.

Swan:
Class: Aves, Family: Anatidae, Genus: *Cygnus*

American robin:
Class: Aves, Family: Turdidae, Genus: *Turdus*

For example, the class Aves, or Birds, is one of the classes in the Animal Kingdom. All birds have beaks, feathers and two legs. They lay hard-shelled eggs and have wings (though not all birds can fly).

Blue-footed booby:
Class: Aves, Family: Sulidae, Genus: *Sula*

IS IT A BIRD?

If a scientist discovers an animal with these features, it's definitely a bird, and belongs in Aves. To work out its family and genus, the scientist would then look at more detailed features, and compare it with other birds to see which it was most similar to (see the three examples above).

Sometimes, biologists also study and compare the DNA of living things (see left), as a way to find out how closely related they are.

THIS DOESN'T FIT!

If scientists discover a living thing that doesn't fit into any existing category, they sometimes have to create a new category. This means the classification system is always growing and changing.

YOU WILL NEED:

A pen and paper

SCIENCE EXPERIMENT:

BE A BIOLOGIST

Sort out the living things into the right categories in the classification tree. To help you, you might have to do some research to find out the features of each category.

Ask

How do you decide which categories a living things belongs in?

CATEGORIES

- amphibians
- arachnids
- birds
- cephalopods
- crustaceans
- fish
- flowering plants
- gastropods
- insects
- mammals
- non-flowering plants
- reptiles

Test

- Look at each of the living things below, and see if you can work out which category each belongs in (without checking on the Internet!). The categories are listed on the right and some hints* and a simplified diagram of the classification tree are below to help you.

axolotl   rose   platypus   flea   octopus   penguin

sea turtle   slug   scorpion   woodlouse   seahorse   moss

*Hints: the word 'gastropod' comes from the Greek for 'stomach-foot'. The word 'cephalopod' comes from the Greek for 'head-foot'.

Observe

How do you make your decisions? Which creatures are the most difficult to classify?

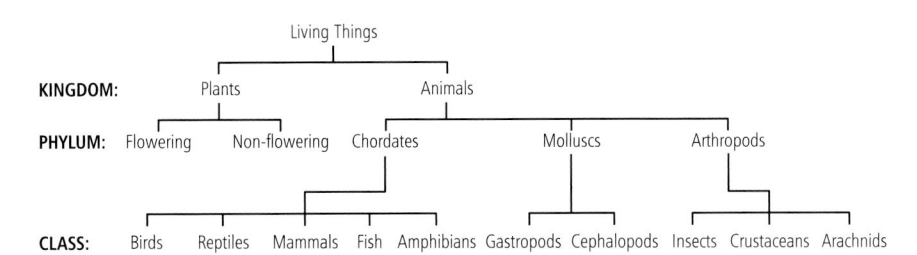

		Living Things						
KINGDOM:	Plants		Animals					
PHYLUM:	Flowering Non-flowering	Chordates		Molluscs		Arthropods		
CLASS:	Birds Reptiles Mammals Fish Amphibians			Gastropods Cephalopods		Insects Crustaceans Arachnids		

Measure

How many did you get right? The answers are on page 32.

WHAT NEXT?

Do some research to find out about new species that have only been discovered in the last ten years. What kind of living things are they?

BODY PLANS

Have you ever noticed that some animals seem to share human features? A monkey, a rat and a squirrel all have hands a bit like ours that can hold food. You can often tell how a dog feels from its facial expression, just like you can with a human friend.

Because living things evolve from other living things, they often share similar features. Even animals that are very different, and belong to separate groups or categories, often have a similar body plan.

Shark skeleton

skull

neck

upper limbs

ribs

tail

finger-like parts

lower limbs

toe-like parts

Human skeleton

MATCHING PARTS

For example, humans and birds are very different, but their skeletons show that they have the same basic body plan.

Ostrich skeleton

LEFTOVER TAIL

Humans don't have tails, but our skeletons have a tailbone. As we evolved from monkey-like animals and moved from the trees to the ground, our tails shrank, as we didn't really need them. The tailbone is all that is left. A leftover, unused body part like this is called a 'vestigial' part.

YOU WILL NEED:

A pen and paper

SCIENCE EXPERIMENT:
LIVING RELATIVES

When you look at different animals' skeletons, their body plans can reveal how closely related they are. Scientists use this to help classify some types of living things.

ASK Can skeletons reveal which species are our closest relatives?

A crab's skeleton is its hard shell and it is on the outside of its body. It is called an exoskeleton.

TEST

- Look at the animal skeletons below.
- Which do you think is our closest relative, and why?

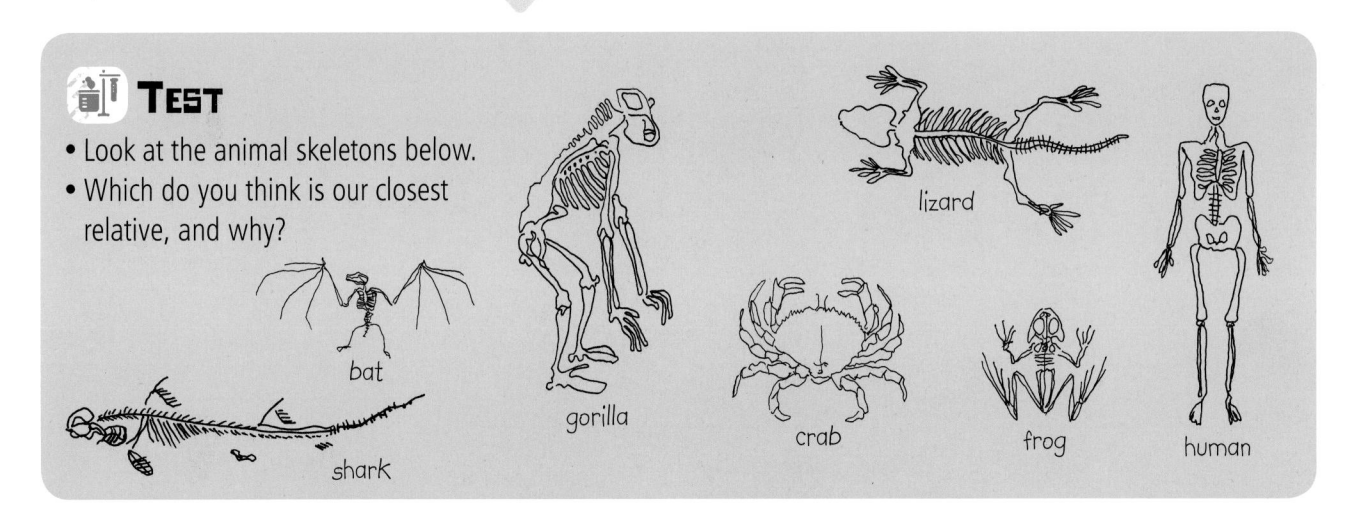

bat

shark

gorilla

lizard

crab

frog

human

OBSERVE

Look for similarities in body structure and parts. Can you spot parallels to our hands, arms or legs in some of the skeletons and not others?

MEASURE

Can you arrange the skeletons in order of how closely they are related to humans? You can find out if you were right on page 32.

WHAT NEXT?

Look up more animal body shapes and skeletons. Can you find out which is our closest animal relative of all?

A frog's skeleton is made up of 159 bones. A human skeleton has 206 bones.

THE DNA KEY

Evolution 'selects' the most useful features in living things. This can only happen because living things are all slightly different, even within the same species. That's because each individual has its own, unique set of genes inside its cells.

COPYING ERRORS

Genes are made of the chemical DNA. When cells divide or living things reproduce, the DNA is copied so that new cells can be made. As this happens, mistakes called mutations can occur in the copies. These mutations make each individual slightly different.

To copy itself, a strand of DNA separates into two halves. Each half builds up a new other half, making two new full strands.

It's possible to see strands of DNA with the naked eye when they are removed from their cells.

DNA FROM A BANANA

Ask an adult to use the surgical spirit. Never use it by yourself or put it in your mouth as it can be dangerous.

YOU WILL NEED:

Freezer
Surgical spirit (from a chemist)
A banana and a fork
Washing-up liquid • Water
Bowl • Sieve
A teaspoon and a tablespoon
A tall glass or jar

DNA is found in the cells of living things, including food plants. It's normally inside the cells, but this experiment lets you release it and see it.

Ask

How can you extract DNA from a banana?

Test

- First, ask an adult to put the surgical spirit in the freezer for a day, to get it really cold.
- Peel the banana, put it in the bowl and mash it well with the fork.
- Add two teaspoons of washing-up liquid and two tablespoons of water and stir in gently.
- Leave the mixture for 10 minutes, then use a spoon to push it through the sieve and collect the liquid in the glass.
- Ask an adult to gently pour in the same amount of cold surgical spirit as there is liquid in the glass and leave for 20 minutes.

DNA strands

Observe

After 20 minutes, there should be a white, lumpy substance at the top of the liquid. This is the DNA. Use the fork to lift bits out.

Measure

DNA is string-shaped (see p. 26), but the strings often coil up into lumps. How long are the longest strings you can see?

WHAT NEXT?

Find out how long all the DNA in a human body is, if it were all stretched out.

The 3D shape of DNA is called a double helix. The word 'helix' comes from the Greek word for 'twisted ' or 'curved'.

READING YOUR RESULTS

When scientists do experiments, they get results. Even if nothing happened as they expected, that is a result too! All results can be useful, but it is important to understand them. Here are some guidelines that scientists use to learn from their results.

USE A CONTROL

In the Toe Test experiment on p. 19, the group of unrelated friends is the control. A control is a normal version of the set-up, without the thing that is being tested. So if you are testing a group of relatives, you need to compare it with another group, who are not related to each other.

Apart from the thing being tested, the control version must match the test version in every way. So, for example, both groups must have the same number of people in them. Then you know that any differences in your results are down to one group being related.

REPEAT AND VERIFY

An experiment may work well once, but what if that was a fluke? So that they can be sure of their results, scientists often repeat an experiment several times to verify their results.

CHECK FOR BIAS

If you're *really* hoping for an exciting result, it's possible you might accidentally-on-purpose 'help' your experiment along by ignoring something that doesn't fit with what you wanted. This is called 'bias' and can happen without you even realising it.

OUTLIERS

What if you were conducting the Delicious or Gross experiment on p. 13, and one of your test subjects gave vomit a rating of 10 out of 10 for deliciousness?

This would be very unexpected and hard to explain. This kind of unusual result is called an outlier. When scientists find outliers, they have to think about whether to discount them from the experiment, or change their experiments to include them. In this case, it might be that the person doing the test didn't understand the rating system. You might decide to double-check this and try again.

KEEPING RECORDS

Writing down the details of each experiment and what the results were is essential for scientists. Not only does it help explain their work to others; it also means they can use results to look for patterns. For example, you might find that the DNA from a Banana experiment on p. 27 works better with very ripe bananas, or with unripe ones.

MAKING MISTAKES

If you spot a mistake, start the experiment again. It would be an even bigger mistake to use the results from a badly run experiment.

However, if a mistake makes something interesting happen, you could set up a new experiment to test for that instead. Important discoveries have been made this way. For example, sticky notes were invented when an inventor was trying to make extra-strong glue, but accidentally created a very weak glue instead.

GLOSSARY

adapt To change to become well-suited to a habitat.

amphibian A cold-blooded animal with a backbone. They usually breathe through gills as young and breathe air as adults.

bacteria A type of tiny single-celled living thing.

biologist An expert in biology.

biology The study of life and living things.

blubber The thick layer of fat found under the skin of some sea animals, such as seals.

bone marrow The soft, fatty substance inside large bones.

calories Units of energy, which are used to measure the amount of energy contained in food.

camouflage Markings, shapes or colours that blend in with the surroundings.

classification Sorting living things out into different types, groups and species.

convergent evolution Evolution of similar traits or features in living things that are not closely related.

DNA (deoxyribonucleic acid) The long, spiral-shaped chemical that genes are made from.

evolution A process of gradual change over steps or generations.

extinct No longer existing.

fossil Rock that has formed the shape of a long-dead living thing or its bones

generation A group of living things that live at the same time. Their children are the next generation, their grandchildren are the generation after that, and so on.

genes Sections of DNA containing instructions that tell cells what to do and control how a living thing grows and works.

genetic trait A feature that is passed on from parents to children by genes.

geology The study of rocks and the Earth.

germs Tiny organisms that cause disease.

habitat The natural home or surroundings of a living thing.

'in the field' When scientists study in wild or natural environments, rather than in a lab.

Latin The language of ancient Rome and its empire. It is widely used in science.

mammal A warm-blooded animal with a backbone that breathes air, has hair and drinks its mother's milk when it is young.

marsupial A mammal that grows inside a pouch on its mother's body when it is very young.

mate Mating happens when a male and female living thing meet to join their reproductive cells together in order to reproduce. A 'mate' also means an animal that another animal mates with.

natural selection The way features that help living things to survive are selected for by evolution.

organ A body part, such as the heart or liver, which performs a job.

posture The way in which you hold your body when standing or sitting; a pose.

predator A living thing that hunts and eats other living things.

prehensile tail A tail that can hold or hang onto objects.

prehistoric From the time before history was written down.

prey A living thing that is eaten by another living thing.

protein An essential part of the diet of many living things that helps build strong muscles and other body parts.

reflex An automatic body reaction that has evolved to help a living thing survive.

reproduce To have babies or offspring so that a species can continue.

reptile A cold-blooded animal with a backbone that usually has dry, scaly skin.

rodent A small mammal with sharp teeth for gnawing, such as a rat or squirrel.

scales Hard plates that overlap to protect the skin of reptiles and some fish.

sexual selection The way features that help living things to win a mate are selected for by evolution.

species The scientific name for a particular type of living thing.

virus A type of tiny germ that can cause some types of diseases.

vitamin An essential part of the diet of many living things, which provides a special type of nutrition and helps growth.

BOOKS

Evolution: The Whole Life on Earth Story by Glenn Murphy (Macmillan)

What is Evolution? by Louise Spilsbury (Wayland)

Evolution Revolution Dr Robert Winston (Dorling Kindersley)

The Story of You by Anna Claybourne (Wayland)

Living Processes: Animal Variation and Classification by Carol Ballard (Wayland)

Straightforward with Science: Classification and Evolution by Peter Riley (Franklin Watts)

Other books in this series:

Science Skills Sorted: Plants
Science Skills Sorted: Human and Animal Bodies
Science Skills Sorted: Habitats
Science Skills Sorted: Life Cycles
Science Skills Sorted: Rocks and Fossils

WEBSITES

Brainpop: Scientific method
https://www.brainpop.com/science/scientificinquiry/scientificmethod/

Science Channel: Charles Darwin
http://www.sciencechannel.com/games-and-interactives/charles-darwin-game/

BBC Bitesize: Theory of Evolution
http://www.bbc.co.uk/schools/gcsebitesize/science/21c_pre_2011/evolution/theoryevolutionrev2.shtml

Science Kids: Biology
http://www.sciencekids.co.nz/biology.html

Interactive Tree of Life
http://www.wellcometreeoflife.org/interactive/

Every effort has been made by the Publishers to ensure that the websites in this book are suitable for children, that they are of the highest educational value, and that they contain no inappropriate or offensive material. However, because of the nature of the Internet, it is impossible to guarantee that the contents of these sites will not be altered. We strongly advise that Internet access is supervised by a responsible adult.

INDEX

ANSWERS

P.15. CREATURE FEATURES:

Hot, sandy desert: big ears • burrowing claws • closable nostrils • furry feet • golden fur
Open ocean: blowhole • flippers • inflatable body parts • torpedo-shaped body • triangle-shaped tail
Snowy forest: big feet • sharp claws • small ears • thick fur • white feathers
Don't worry if your answers don't match these ones, sometimes there is more than one right answer. Here are some examples:
• Closable nostrils are used by some desert animals to keep sand out of their noses, but they are also used by marine mammals, such as seals, when they dive underwater.
• Some desert animals have fur on the bottom of their feet to protect their feet from hot surfaces, but polar bears also have furry feet to protect their feet from cold surfaces.
• Camels have big feet that help them walk on soft sand. Snowshoe hares also have big feet compared to the size of their bodies. Their big feet help spread their body weight and stop them sinking into deep snow.

P. 23. BE A BIOLOGIST:

amphibians: axolotl • arachnids: scorpion • birds: penguin • cephalopods: octopus • crustaceans: woodlouse • fish: seahorse • flowering plants: rose • gastropods: slug • insects: flea • mammals: platypus • non-flowering plants: moss • reptiles: sea turtle

P. 25. LIVING RELATIVES:

The order of our animal relatives from closest to furthest is: gorilla, bat, lizard, frog, shark, crab.

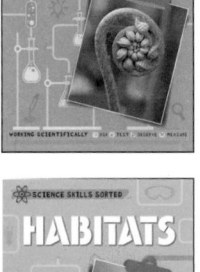

SCIENCE SKILLS SORTED

These are the lists of contents for the titles in the Science Skills Sorted series:

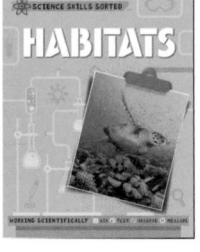

PLANTS

What makes a plant a plant? • The science of plants • Working scientifically • Seeds • Plant defence • What plants need to grow • Surviving a drought • Water content • How leaves work • Helping nature • Flowers and seeds • Autumn colours • Cloning plants • Reading your results • Glossary and further information • Index

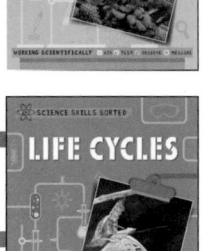

HABITATS

What is a habitat? • The science of habitats • Working scientifically • Wildlife habitats • Adaptations • Moving in • Blending in • Extreme habitats • Keystone species • How trees help • Balancing the numbers • Building the environment • Climate change • Reading your results • Glossary and further information • Index

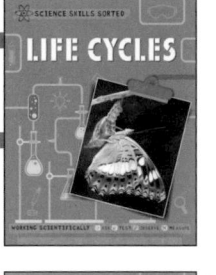

LIFE CYCLES

What is a life cycle? • The science of life cycles • Working scientifically • From seed to seed • Eggs and babies • Metamorphosis • Finding a mate • Dividing bacteria • Budding yeast • Spreading out • Generations • Life cycle maths • Hitching a ride • Reading your results • Glossary and further information • Index

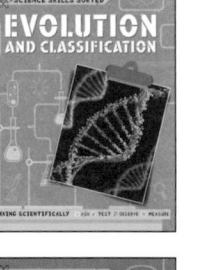

EVOLUTION AND CLASSIFICATION

What is evolution? • The science of evolution • Working scientifically • Evolution in action • Survival of the fittest • Finding food • Adapting to habitats • Winning a mate • Genes and genetic traits • Classification • Sorting it out • Body plans • The DNA key • Reading your results • Glossary and further information • Index

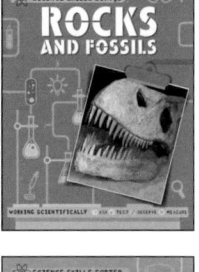

ROCKS AND FOSSILS

What are rocks, minerals and fossils? • The science of rocks and fossils • Working scientifically • Types of rock • Rocks and water • Minerals and crystals • How hard? • Weathering and erosion • Expanding ice • Making mountains • Volcanoes and earthquakes • How fossils form • Fossil puzzles • Reading your results • Glossary and further information • Index

HUMAN AND ANIMAL BODIES

Humans and other animals? • Studying humans and animals • Working scientifically • Bones • Moving on land • Built to fly • Super streamlined • Sharp sight • Locating sound • Interesting smell • Teeth and beaks • Breathing • Unique individuals • Reading your results • Glossary and further information • Index